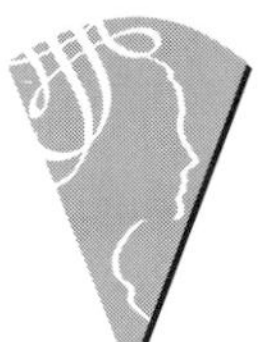

Air & Space

Broadcasting & Journalism

Business & Industry

Entertainment & Performing Arts

Government & Politics

Literature

Science & Medicine

Sports & Athletics

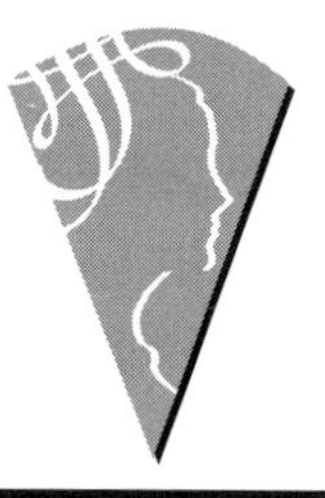

FEMALE FIRSTS IN THEIR FIELDS

LITERATURE

Virginia Aronson

Introduction by
Roslyn Rosen

CHELSEA HOUSE PUBLISHERS
Philadelphia

Produced by P. M. Gordon Associates, Inc.
Philadelphia, Pennsylvania

Editor in Chief Stephen Reginald
Managing Editor James D. Gallagher
Production Manager Pamela Loos
Art Director Sara Davis
Director of Photography Judy L. Hasday
Senior Production Editor Lisa Chippendale
Publishing Coordinator James McAvoy

Picture research by Artemis Picture Research Group, Inc.
Cover illustration by Cliff Spohn
Cover design by Keith Trego

Frontispiece: Toni Morrison

The Chelsea House World Wide Web site address is
http://www.chelseahouse.com

First Printing

1 3 5 7 9 8 6 4 2

Library of Congress Cataloging-in-Publication Data

Aronson, Virginia.
Female firsts in their fields. Literature / Virginia Aronson.
p. cm.
Includes bibliographical references and index.
Summary: Discusses the lives and literary characters of six American women writers–Judy Blume, Pearl Buck, Toni Morrison, Alice Walker, Edith Wharton, and Phyllis Wheatley.
ISBN 0-7910-5146-3 (hardcover)
1. Women authors, American–Biography–Juvenile literature.
2. Women and literature–United States–Juvenile literature.
[1. Authors, American. 2. American literature–Collections.
3. Women–Biography.] I. Title.
PS147.A76 1998
810.9'9287–dc21
[B]

98-44004
CIP
AC

CONTENTS

Introduction 7

CHAPTER 1
Phillis Wheatley 11

CHAPTER 2
Edith Wharton 19

CHAPTER 3
Pearl S. Buck 27

CHAPTER 4
Judy Blume 37

CHAPTER 5
Toni Morrison 45

CHAPTER 6
Alice Walker 53

Chronology 62

Further Reading 63

Index 64

INTRODUCTION

Roslyn Rosen

When I was a toddler, it struck me that the other people in my family's New York apartment building were different. They did not use their hands when they talked, and they did not have to watch each other speak. I had been born deaf, and I felt sorry for them because they did not know the joy of drawing pictures in the air. They could not splash ideas into the air with a jab of the finger or a wave of the hand. Not until later did I realize the downside of being deaf–I couldn't communicate directly with my grandparents and extended family members, I depended on others to make important phone calls for me, and I found life's opportunities narrower, in part because I had few deaf (let alone female) role models.

Gallaudet University in Washington, D.C., is the only college for deaf students in the world. I arrived there in September 1958. It was a haven where sign language was part of the educational process, where there were deaf professors, and where opportunities for extracurricular leadership abounded. At Gallaudet I met deaf female professionals for the first time, although there were probably not more than three or four. The president and administrators of Gallaudet were all males who could hear–typical of school administrations during those years.

In my first month at Gallaudet, I also met the man who would become my husband. My destiny was charted: major in something that I could use as a homemaker (since that would be my job), get married, have a bunch of kids, and live happily ever after. This was the expectation for women in the late 1950s and early 1960s. And I stuck to the script: I majored in art with an emphasis on education and English, got married, and had three children. My life was complete–or so I thought.

The 1960s were turbulent and thought-provoking years. The civil rights movement and the beginnings of a women's movement emphasized human rights and equality for all. I came to see how alike the issues were that faced women, people of color, and people with disabilities, in terms of human rights and respect for human differences. Multicultural studies are vital for this understanding. Changes were occurring at an accelerating rate. Those changes affected my husband and me by broadening our traditional gender roles. With my husband's support, I pursued a master's degree in education of deaf students and later a doctoral degree in education administration. From my first job as a part-time sign language teacher, I eventually joined the faculty at Gallaudet University. In 1981 I was promoted to dean of the College for Continuing Education, and in 1993, to vice president for academic affairs.

During the formative years of my career, many of my role models and mentors were deaf men who had reached positions of leadership. They hired, taught, advised, and encouraged me. There were times when I felt the effects of the "glass ceiling" (an invisible barrier that keeps women or minorities from rising any higher). Sometimes I needed to depend on my male colleagues because my access to "old boy" networks or decision makers was limited. When I became involved with the National Association of the Deaf (NAD), the world's oldest organization of deaf people, I met deaf women who became role models–Dr. Gertie Galloway was the first deaf female president of the NAD, and Marcella Meyer had founded the Greater Los Angeles Community Service of the Deaf (GLAD). In 1980 I was elected to the board of directors of the National Association of the Deaf, and in 1990, I became the second woman elected president of NAD.

When I became a dean at Gallaudet in 1981, I also became a member of the school's Council of Deans, which at the time included only two deaf deans and two female deans. I was the only deaf woman dean. The vice president was a white male, and he once commented that top administrators often build management teams in their own image. I have found that to be true. As a dean, I was the highest-ranking deaf woman at Gallaudet, and I was able to hire and help a number of young deaf female professionals within the College for Continuing Education and our regional centers around the country. In the five years that I have been vice president at Gallaudet I have added many deaf, female, and minority members to my own management team. When I was the president of NAD, I hired its first deaf female executive director, Nancy Bloch. I also encouraged two of my friends, Mabs Holcomb and Sharon Wood, to write the first deaf women history book, a source of inspiration for young deaf girls.

It is important for women who have reached the top levels of their fields to advise and help younger women to become successful. It is also important for young girls to know about the groundbreaking contributions of women who came before them. The women profiled in this series of biographies overcame many obstacles to succeed. Some had physical handicaps, others fought generations of discriminatory attitudes toward women in the workplace. The world may never provide equal opportunities for every human being, but we can all work together to improve life for the next generation.

DR. ROSLYN ROSEN is the Vice President for Academic Affairs at Gallaudet University in Washington, D.C. Dr. Rosen has served as a board member and President of the National Association of the Deaf (NAD), the oldest consumer organization in the world, and was a member of the National Captioning Institute's executive board for nine years. She is currently a board member of the World Federation of the Deaf. Dr. Rosen also wears the hats of daughter, wife, mother, and proud grandmother.

Phillis Wheatley, Negro Servant to Mr. John Wheatley, of Boston.

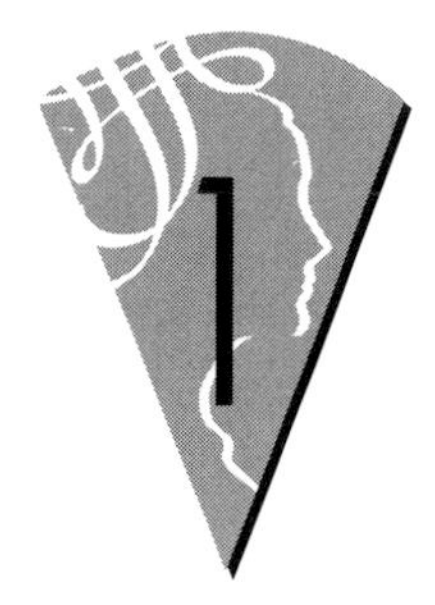

PHILLIS WHEATLEY

On July 11, 1761, the slave ship *Phillis* arrived in the Boston harbor with between 70 and 80 young African women and children squeezed on board. Many of the travelers had died on the way, some from hunger, others by throwing themselves overboard. At that time, nearly 600 slaves lived in Boston, most working as house servants.

John and Susanna Wheatley, a wealthy Boston couple who owned a number of slaves, went down to the dock that day to "purchase" a girl to help with household chores. Susanna named her after the slave ship, Phillis.

John Wheatley was a successful tailor and merchant who owned warehouses, wharves, a merchant schooner, a shop, and a number of houses. The Wheatleys lived in a busy section of Boston with their twins, 18-year-old Mary and Nathaniel. Mary wanted to be a teacher, so she took Phillis under her wing and began to teach her the English language.

Phillis was a natural student, quick and eager, and within a few months she was reading. Within a year and a half, she "attained the English Language . . . to such Degree as to read

An engraving of Phillis Wheatley originally published in England in 1773 with her book of poems.

This old illustration portrays a slave ship similar to the one that brought Phillis Wheatley to North America.

any, the most difficult Parts, of the Sacred Writings," according to John Wheatley. After the Bible, Phillis moved on to the other books in the Wheatley home. The Wheatleys borrowed books for Phillis from their well-to-do friends.

Phillis soon learned to write. Popular public opinion at the time held that girls were not to be schooled, brought up instead to serve as wives and mothers. Many people believed that blacks could not or should not be educated, and in southern towns it was against the law to teach an African American how to write. Thus, Phillis was doubly fortunate to live with the Wheatleys, where her intelligence was recognized and valued, her efforts to learn encouraged and supported. They made sure that she had an adequate supply of writing paper, ink, and quill pens, as well as candles since she usually wrote at night.

Around the age of 12, Phillis began to compose poetry. Because she could read Latin and Greek, she had been enjoying the long story-like poems of the Greek writer Homer. But her favorite poet was

Alexander Pope, who wrote long poems called "elegies," usually in honor of someone who had died. Her own first poem was "On the Death of the Rev. Dr. Sewell when Sick, 1765," an elegy to the pastor of the Old South Church she attended (who actually did not die until several years later, and who spelled his name "Sewall").

Phillis herself was not healthy and suffered from asthma, which caused coughing and difficulty in breathing. Phillis was not required to do much more than light housework, and the Wheatleys regularly took her with them to the clean air of the countryside.

The inspiration for Phillis's writing came from both her strong religious ideas and the political activities of the day. Since she was a slave, her feelings on the value of freedom ran deep. She began to write poetry in favor of the American colonists who argued, then battled, for freedom from British rule.

At the age of 13, Phillis composed one of her best-known poems, "To the University of Cambridge, in New England," in which she celebrated learning, virtue, and Christianity, the basic themes of most of her writing. In December 1767, her first published poem appeared in the newspaper, the *Newport Mercury*.

In the fall of 1770, Phillis wrote an elegy after the death of the Reverend George Whitefield, which was printed and sold in Boston, New York, Philadelphia, and Britain. An advertisement in the *Massachusetts Spy* at the time read: "An Elegiac Poem, on the Death of the Celebrated Divine . . . by PHILLIS, a Servant girl of 17 years of Age, Belonging to Mr. J. WHEATLEY . . . but 9 Years in this Country from Africa."

Phillis sent a copy of the poem to the Countess of Huntingdon in Britain, for whom the deceased reverend had served as private clergyman: "The occasion of my addressing your Ladiship will, I hope, apologize for this my boldness in doing it: it is to enclose a few lines on the decease of your worthy chaplain."

Phillis continued to write elegies and, by the fall of 1772, had begun to read and recite poetry for gatherings at the Wheatleys and in the homes of their influential friends. Regarded as a curiosity, a genius, or an anomaly by some, Phillis gained more and more public attention and was widely praised for her modesty, piety, and wit. Soon, certain antislavery voices began to speak out about Phillis, pointing to the poet as living proof that black people could and should be educated, allowed to attain their full potential and to prove their intellectual capability and equality.

Susanna had been attempting to find a publisher for a book of Phillis's poems. She even collected the signatures of 18 of Boston's most important citizens, who confirmed that Phillis Wheatley, a slave girl, was indeed the author of the collection. This "affidavit," later published in Phillis's book, included the signatures of Governor Hutchinson and John Hancock.

In the meantime, the Countess of Huntingdon, a patron of good causes, published the poem Phillis had sent to her. The countess then met with Archibald Bell, London's foremost bookseller and printer, who had received Phillis's writings and the affidavit from Susanna. John Wheatley praised Phillis in an enclosed letter, remarking, "As to her Writing, her own Curiosity led her to it." The countess decided to help Phillis publish her book.

In the spring of 1773, the Wheatleys sent Phillis to Britain with Nathaniel, who was traveling between continents on business. Phillis had been ill,

A portrait of Wheatley from her brief period of recognition, between the publication of her poems and her decline into poverty.

and the doctors advised sea air. Before her voyage, she composed the poem "Farewell to America," which was printed in newspapers hailing her as "the extraordinary negro poetess" and "the ingenius negro poet."

Phillis enjoyed her brief visit to London, where the countess arranged for her to meet a number of powerful people, including Benjamin Franklin, who was there as a spokesperson for the American colonies. She even had an appointment to meet King George, but she became ill before the meeting and was called home.

On September 16, 1773, the London *Chronicle* announced the publication of Phillis Wheatley's book, *Poems on Various Subjects, Religious and*

Moral, in England. Phillis was 20 years old, the first black American to publish a book. (Only one other American woman, another poet, had published a book.) Some book reviewers used the opportunity to speak out against the practice of slavery. John Wheatley granted Phillis her freedom.

Unfortunately, Phillis had little else besides her freedom. And, with the political upheaval between Britain and the colonies, her income from the sales of her book was meager. So she stayed on at the Wheatleys, nursing Susanna until her death in March 1774. Phillis wrote to a friend, "Let us imagine the loss of a parent, sister or brother, the tenderness of all these were united in her. . . . I was treated by her more like her child than her servant."

By April 1775, the Revolutionary War had officially started, and Phillis was living with Mary and her family in Providence, Rhode Island. In October of that year, she wrote a letter to George Washington, the commander-in-chief of the colonial army, enclosing a poem in praise of his efforts. Washington wrote back, inviting her to visit him, which she did soon after she read his kind words about her "elegant lines," "poetical talents," and "genius . . . a person so favored by the Muses" (which means blessed with artistic talent).

When John Wheatley died in the spring of 1778, Phillis, who had returned to Boston, married John Peters, a freed slave. Peters had, at various times, worked as a grocer, a baker, and a barber. Historical records in Massachusetts indicate that he also appeared in courts of law to defend other black people. The newlyweds moved into a house on what was then Queen Street in Boston.

Mary died the following fall, around the time Phillis became pregnant with her first child. She had begun to collect her newer poems for a second book, which she planned to dedicate to Benjamin Franklin. Despite the newspaper ads for this collection of 33 poems and 13 letters, Phillis was unable to secure a publisher, largely because few people had enough money to buy books in the midst of the war.

After the war ended in 1781, Peters opened a shop in downtown Boston. The business failed, forcing him into debt and confinement in a debtors' prison. By that time, Phillis had borne two more children, but only the youngest had survived.

Ill and penniless, Phillis moved into a dilapidated boarding house for poor blacks, where she worked as a cleaning woman to pay for her lodging. On December 5, 1784, Phillis Wheatley, age 31, died in her bed with her infant in her arms. (Her baby also died.) She had continued to write poems, even in her final months. A few days after her death, Phillis Wheatley's poem "Liberty and Peace" was published in Boston.

Poems on Various Subjects, Religious and Moral was not published in the United States until two years after Phillis's death, but the book has been reprinted many times since. During the 1800s, the abolitionists frequently referred to Wheatley's work in their attempts to abolish slavery. Her poem "Reply" (1775) is the first known literary work in which an African American celebrates her heritage.

Her accomplishments were fully recognized when, in 1985, the governor of Massachusetts declared February 1 as "Phillis Wheatley Day." Sometimes referred to as "the mother of black literature in America," Phillis is now widely recognized as an important American poet.

EDITH WHARTON

Few people today know much more about Edith Wharton than that she wrote the book *The Age of Innocence*, on which the popular 1993 film was based. But in her day, from the turn of the century until her death in 1937, Edith Wharton was one of the most popular novelists alive. Her books were instant bestsellers, and she lived the life of a celebrity in her two homes in France.

Born on January 24, 1862, Edith Newbold Jones grew up on West 23rd Street in New York City, the only daughter of George Frederic and Lucretia Stevens Rhinelander Jones. Her two brothers were more than a dozen years older, so Edith was treated like an only child. She regarded her childhood as "safe, guarded, monotonous . . . well-ordered and well-to-do."

Edith's grandfather, William Rhinelander, was a multimillionaire, enabling Edith and her family to live in luxury on their inheritance. They were considered "old money" (versus the "new rich" who earned their millions themselves),

Edith Wharton, one of the most popular novelists of the early 20th century, grew up among wealthy New Yorkers, whose society she found stifling.

and none of these New York "aristocrats" ever worked. Edith felt confined in this closed society of extremely wealthy people who emphasized good manners and good taste but ignored or discouraged interest in the arts and any display of excess–including high emotion or deep passion.

When Edith was around four years old, a national economic depression reduced the Jones family income. George Jones moved the family to Europe, where they traveled throughout Italy, France, and Germany for six years. Edith's father taught her to read and hired tutors so that she could learn the language of each country in which they lived. Edith was especially fond of the colorful beauty of Rome, and fell in love with Paris, where she began to create stories so real she felt "swept off in a sea of dreams."

Edith was certainly a child of privilege, yet she was a lonely, unhappy little girl. Her mother, Edith believed, was harshly critical and unloving, and the society in which she was raised disapproved of her natural inclinations: Edith loved books and stories, art and beauty, the life of the creative imagination. At that time, girls of Edith's social class were not educated, nor were they expected to work or to think deeply. "Well-to-do" women behaved "nicely," that is, they married, bore children, and entertained their passionless peers. Edith conformed outwardly, while secretly cultivating her hungry mind.

When she was around 10 years old, Edith was allowed to read the books in her father's library, a room she later described as "a sea of wonders." There, she read much of the Bible, the works of the great poets like Shelley and Keats, and all of Shakespeare's plays. At age 11, she began to write her first novel. Edith's mother discouraged her pursuit of writing at once, but when she was 16, Edith somehow convinced her parents to print a volume of poetry she had written.

At 18, she moved to Italy with her parents but, after her father's death, resettled in New York. When she was 23, Edith married 35-year-old Edward "Teddy" Wharton, a wealthy Harvard graduate who typified the rich aristocrats of her circle: Teddy was charming and loved to travel, but he was completely bored by art, literature, and work.

The marriage was not a happy one and Edith felt lonely, her creativity stifled. To her lifelong regret, the couple failed to have children. In order to overcome her loneliness and depression, Edith began to write again, creating an imaginary world to help her defeat a "paralyzing melancholy."

After publishing some poems and short stories in the popular magazines of the day, such as *Harper's* and *Scribner's,* Edith turned her energies to the renovation and decoration of the Whartons' homes in Manhattan and Newport. Edith soon collaborated with the young architect Ogden Codman Jr., on a book, *The Decoration of Houses.*

One of the first books about home design published in the United States, *The Decoration of Houses* advocated the simple, uncluttered style of home decorating then popular in Italy and France. The book was a great success, launching a new trend in American home decorating and selling steadily for 40 years.

The fact that her first book was instantly popular and continued to sell "from edition to edition" inspired Wharton to continue her writing. She next published *The Greater Inclination,* her first collection of short stories. Readers and critics raved, and Wharton became a celebrity.

In 1901, the Whartons built The Mount, an elegant retreat home near Lennox, Massachusetts, which Edith designed herself. Often writing longhand in bed, Edith loved working at The Mount, where she "lived and gardened and wrote contentedly" for the next 10 years. At The Mount Edith began to form a circle of like-minded friends, intellectual, literary people who enjoyed discussing books and reading poetry together. Henry James, the American-born author of such classics as *The Wings of the Dove* and *The Portrait of a Lady,* visited Edith at The Mount from his self-imposed exile in Europe.

James advised Wharton to "Do New York!"–that is, to write novels about the rarified subset of society in which she was raised. Wharton took her friend's advice, creating what is regarded as her first masterpiece, the novel *House of Mirth.* Set in the wealthy, close-minded New York upper class of her own youth, Wharton's *House of Mirth* clearly illustrates how oppressive the social system was for women. Published in 1905, the book was a controversial bestseller and marked first of a series of highly regarded Wharton classics, including *Ethan Frome* and *The Custom of the Country.*

After 22 years of tolerating a marriage without passion, at 45 Edith Wharton fell in love for the first time. A friend of Henry James, Morton Fullerton was a 42-year-old Harvard graduate, an American journalist who lived in England and wrote for the London *Times.* Although the affair cooled after a few years, Edith divorced Teddy in 1913, after 28 years of marriage. By this time, Teddy had become mentally unstable, the Mount had been sold, and Edith had moved to Europe, where she would make her home for the remainder of her life.

As a single woman, Edith discovered the joy of personal liberation. She felt free for the first time in her life, traveling extensively with friends and splitting her productive writing time between her two lovely French homes, one just outside Paris and the other on the Riviera. Henry James began to affectionately refer to Wharton as "the whirling princess."

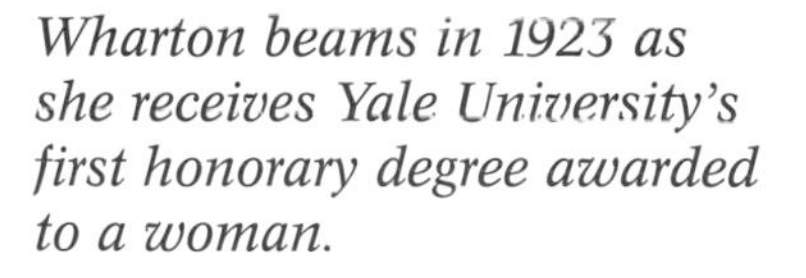
Wharton beams in 1923 as she receives Yale University's first honorary degree awarded to a woman.

During World War I (1914–18), Edith devoted herself to assisting the homeless refugees who poured into Paris, establishing hostels for displaced families and organizing medical clinics, free kitchens, and an employment agency for the poor. She housed more than 700 war orphans in six different residences at her own expense. Before the war ended, France and Belgium had both thanked Edith for her generous, selfless work, decorating her with their highest honors, the Cross of the Legion of Honor and the Chevalier of the Order of Leopold.

After the war ended, Wharton published *The Age of Innocence,* another New York society novel full of fascinating characters, many based on the people who had made her own childhood so miserable. Published in 1920, the book was a popular and critical success, receiving the Pulitzer Prize for fiction in 1921. Wharton was the first female to receive this coveted literary award given annually by Columbia University for the year's most important novel. Because she had sometimes been criticized for her "sordid" plots and "disagreeable" characters, Wharton was amused when she was presented with the Pulitzer Prize and her book was called the one that

Late in her life, Wharton continued to be productive as a writer.

best portrayed "the wholesome atmosphere of American life."

In the last years of her life, Edith Wharton was at the peak of her fame. In 1923 she had become the first female to receive an honorary degree from Yale University. A child of wealth, she succeeded in her drive for financial independence, developing her skill and her following so that she could "live by her pen." A shy woman, almost to the day she died she maintained her high level of visibility with her amazing productivity as a writer.

Soon after her 75th birthday, Wharton answered a young person's query about her age: "It feels pretty good when you get to it." Only a few months later, Edith Wharton suffered a stroke. She died on August 11, 1937, and was buried in Versailles, France.

Publically ignored for several decades, the writings of this talented woman are beginning to once again capture readers' attention, first via Martin Scorsese's opulent motion picture version of *The Age of Innocence.* More recently, an exhibition of artifacts from her life and work at the National Portrait Gallery entitled "Edith Wharton's World in Portraits of People and Places" has brought her into the limelight again. In 1997, *The Decoration of Houses* was reissued, and three more film adaptations of her fiction were in production in Hollywood.

The rich and compelling works of Edith Wharton are coming to light once more, along with the reputation of the author whose work critics have called "among the handsomest achievements in our literature."

PEARL S. BUCK

Not long after her birth in June of 1892, Pearl Comfort Sydenstricker left the little town of Hillsboro, West Virginia, for China, where she would live for most of the next forty years. Her parents, Absalom and Carie Sydenstricker, were Presbyterian missionaries who spent decades attempting to convert the Chinese to a Christian way of life.

During the nineteenth century, Americans knew almost nothing about China, which they viewed as a vast, exotic, distant land. The Chinese people were also unfamiliar to Americans, and many believed in the naive and disparaging stereotypes of Asians as a dishonest, cruel culture with strange costumes and weird customs. In turn, some of the Chinese people Pearl met during her childhood taunted her, ridiculing her as a "little foreign devil" because of her blonde hair and blue eyes.

When Pearl was four, her family moved to Chinkiang, where they lived for many years. Pearl was educated in Chinese by her tutor, Mr. Kung, and in English by her mother.

A humanitarian as well as a writer, Pearl Buck holds one of the Amerasian children she helped rescue from homelessness and hunger.

The Sydenstrickers pose for a family portrait in China, probably in early 1901. In the front row, left to right, are the eight-year-old Pearl; her father, Absalom; her two-year-old sister, Grace; and her mother, Carie. Behind the family stands the governess Amah Wang.

She read hungrily, and her favorite books were those of Charles Dickens, the British author of *A Christmas Carol* and *Oliver Twist*. She often sent stories she wrote herself to an English newspaper, the *Shanghai Mercury*, winning prizes for the best children's submissions. From a young age, Pearl knew that she would be a writer.

Amah Wang, Pearl's Chinese governess (*amah* means "governess"), opened up for Pearl the world of ordinary Chinese people. The two visited herbal doctors and food vendors, and they attended festivals, weddings, funerals, and the local Chinese theater.

By age seven or eight, Pearl was reading English and Chinese literature. She grew up fully bilingual, speaking fluently and writing well in both languages. As an adult, Pearl referred to herself as "mentally bifocal" and "culturally bifocal" because of her natural ability since childhood to live in two very different cultures at the same time.

In 1900, a violent revolution called the Boxer Uprising occurred in China. While Absalom remained behind, Pearl, her mother, and her new baby sister, Grace, fled their home for the safety of Shanghai. They lived there as refugees for a year. Pearl's older brother, Edgar, whom she adored, was sent to live with relatives in America. In July 1901, the rest of the Sydenstricker family set sail for the U.S. as well where they stayed with Carie's family in West Virginia. Pearl enjoyed her time in the lush foothills of the Shenendoah Mountains, but felt disappointed that no one there seemed to be interested in China.

When the Sydenstrickers returned to Chinkiang, Pearl attended a nearby mission school for girls and continued to read every book she could get her hands on. She then moved to Shanghai to go to an English girls' school for a year. During this time, she volunteered at the Door of Hope, a shelter for Chinese slave girls and prostitutes. Pearl taught the girls to sew and knit. They told her their personal stories of the rape, torture, and starvation common in what was then a flourishing sex slave trade. Pearl was angry at the widespread mistreatment of Chinese women and girls.

In 1910, Pearl sailed back to America to go to Randolph-Macon Women's College, where she was greeted by her fellow students as an exotic foreigner. Although she eventually joined a sorority and was later chosen president of her junior class, Pearl continued to feel like an outsider. None of her classmates were in the least bit interested in the Chinese world she had come from.

Pearl was an excellent student. She also published her short stories in the undergraduate literary mag-

Though chased from China by antiforeign sentiment in the 1920s, Buck later urged Congress to repeal the immigration act that excluded Chinese. Here she meets a group of Chinese women after testifying before the House Immigration Committee.

azine and won prizes in writing contests. Upon her graduation in 1914, a psychology professor offered her a position at the college as a teaching assistant, which Pearl accepted. However, she was called back to China to tend to her mother, who was suffering from a tropical disease.

While nursing her dying mother, Pearl taught in a mission school for boys. By February 1917, she had fallen in love and was engaged to a handsome agricultural missionary from America named John Lossing Buck.

Although they were married for 17 years, Pearl

was unhappy almost from the start. She felt that her husband kept her from living her own life. He expected her to be a traditional wife and provided no support for her writing.

By 1924, the Bucks had moved from rural North China, where Pearl observed firsthand the peasant life she would later write about in her most popular books, to the city of Nanking. Both Bucks taught at the University of Nanking, while Pearl tended to their baby, Carol.

When Carol was around 18 months old, Pearl began to fear that the child was not developing normally. By the time Carol was four, Pearl knew that she needed to take her child to medical specialists for a professional diagnosis.

The Bucks traveled to New York, where they attended Cornell University for graduate studies while Pearl took Carol to see various medical specialists. Reluctantly, she began to accept the diagnosis of permanent mental retardation. (Carol was actually suffering from phenylketonuria or "PKU," an inherited disorder we now know how to treat successfully. In the 1920s, the cure, which is based on diet, was unknown.) Since Pearl was unable to have any more children, the Bucks decided to adopt a three-month-old girl, whom they named Janice.

Before returning to China, Pearl's essay, "The Chinese Student Mind," appeared in *The Nation,* and *Asia* magazine accepted her short story "A Chinese Woman Speaks," which described the ancient practice of foot-binding. With this story Pearl began her lifelong advocacy for women's rights and racial tolerance.

When the Bucks returned to China in 1925, violent antiforeign sentiment was sweeping the country. At one point, they were forced to take refuge in the home of one of their Chinese servants, who hid them from the soldiers slaughtering foreigners all over the city. The Bucks fled to Japan, losing everything but the clothes they were wearing. There Pearl began a novel about a poor Chinese farmer named Wang Lung. When they returned to their ransacked home in 1928, Pearl sent her story "A Chinese Woman Speaks" to David Lloyd, a literary agent in New York. She included a new unpublished supplement, suggesting the two together might make a novel, which she wished to call *Winds of Heaven.*

In 1929, Pearl found a comfortable home for Carol in the Vineland Training School located in New Jersey, where she would live for more than 60 years. Pearl never mentioned her daughter when she became a best-selling author and popular public figure only a year or two later.

The small publishing house of John Day offered to print Pearl's book, retitled *East Wind: West Wind.* In choosing to publish Pearl's novel, the publisher, Richard Walsh, challenged what he called "the well-known wall of prejudice against Chinese books."

He soon agreed to publish Pearl's new novel about the farmer Wang Lung, which he suggested they call *The Good Earth.* With her realistic portrayal of an ordinary Chinese peasant family, the first in Western literature, Pearl S. Buck became an overnight sensation: *The Good Earth* sold nearly two million copies and was translated into more than 30 languages. Eventually, the book inspired both a Broadway play and an award-winning Hollywood film.

Pearl was grateful for the financial independence her success guaranteed, but later admitted privately, "I would gladly have written nothing if I could have just an average child in Carol." In order to continue to provide institutional care for her daughter, however, Pearl kept on writing popular novels, mostly about the everyday Chinese life she knew so well.

The first American woman to win the Nobel Prize for Literature, Buck accepts the award from King Gustav of Sweden.

When antiforeign violence erupted again in China in the spring of 1931, Pearl resolved to move to the United States. In July 1933, she asked Lossing for a divorce. Two hours after her divorce was final, Pearl married Richard Walsh, her publisher and, by this time, best friend and lover.

Pearl and Richard soon adopted two infant boys. A year later, they adopted two more babies. Pearl became an outspoken advocate for adoption, creating Welcome House, an agency for children the other adoption agencies neglected: children of mixed races, and minority and handicapped children. She began to rescue as many of what she called "Amer-

Buck in her seventies, still writing and working for humanitarian causes.

asian" children as possible, finding homes for the thousands of offspring of U.S. servicemen and Asian women who ended up homeless and hungry in the war-torn streets of Japan, Korea, and elsewhere. Welcome House was the first international, interracial adoption agency in the United States. It was only the first of a dozen projects Pearl started to support both the welfare of children and international understanding.

When Pearl S. Buck was awarded the Nobel Prize in literature in 1938, she became the first American woman to receive this international honor.

In 1950, Pearl published a brave, honest book about her daughter Carol, *The Child Who Never Grew.* She then became an outspoken, generous supporter of research on and public education about mental retardation.

After a long illness, Pearl's beloved husband, Richard, died in 1960. She never remarried, but continued to publish and to work tirelessly as a humanitarian and human rights advocate. By the time she died of cancer in 1973 at age 80, Pearl S. Buck's body of literary work included over 70 books in virtually every genre, or category, of writing: novels, short stories, plays, biographies, autobiography, journalism, poetry, and children's literature. She also translated into English the classic Chinese novel of over 1,000 pages, *All Men Are Brothers.*

In breaking new ground with her portraits of Asian life, in particular the lives and oppression of Asian women, she almost single-handedly awakened America to both the unique beauty and the suffering that is the real China. Through her writing and her social justice work, Pearl Buck consistently pointed to the similarities of all peoples.

JUDY BLUME

Although Judy Sussman never even fantasized about becoming the famous children's book author Judy Blume, as a child she was surrounded by and greatly influenced by books. Her house was filled with books, and her mother, Esther Sussman, was always immersed in one.

Judy poured through biographies for young people, the popular Nancy Drew mystery series, and books about girls who rode horses. When she was small, her favorite book was *Madeline* by Ludwig Bemelmans.

Like both of her parents, Judy was born and raised in Elizabeth, New Jersey. The Sussmans were a happy family, but as Judy grew older, she began to feel as if she could no longer confide in any of them. "When I was growing up I didn't doubt my parents' love for me, but I didn't think they understood me, or had any idea of what I was like," Judy recalled as an adult. "And I made no effort to try to change that. I just assumed that parents don't understand their kids, ever. That there is a lot of pretending in family life."

Judy was born on February 12, 1938. As a young girl, she

Judy Blume became a best-selling author by focusing on questions she wondered about as a child.

One winter in Florida, Judy staged a ballet for people in her apartment building.

had a lot of questions about life, which she attempted to find answers for in books. Judy wanted to read books about kids like herself, kids with concerns about how life works: What was it like to be an adult? What would growing up feel like? What happened when someone died? At that time, there were no books written for kids that addressed Judy's questions, which she kept to herself.

As a child, Judy spent several winters in Miami, where she once staged a ballet for the residents of her apartment building. Thirty years later, Judy wrote *Starring Sally J. Freedman as Herself* (1977), in which many of the experiences of the protagonist, or main character, were recreated from those Miami winters.

From age 11 to 14, Judy spent summers at an overnight camp in Connecticut, where she finally overcame her fear of swimming. She later wrote about this and other childhood fears in *Otherwise Known as Sheila the Great* (1972).

Judy attended Battin High School, a large public high school for girls, where she was an A student. She worked on the school newspaper, sang in the chorus, and performed in the modern dance troupe. She continued to enjoy writing pop songs, drawing, and illustrating, activities she had begun in the eighth grade. She loved theatre and had a small part in one of her school's plays.

Even though she was dating older boys, Judy recalls that she never talked openly about sex or other personal issues with her family. In fact, Judy was unable to share her real self with anyone. "I felt a lot of pressure to be popular, so I kept the real me hidden, deep inside," she explains.

Judy chose Boston University for a degree in elementary education. During her first week at college, Judy became very ill with mononucleosis, a virus common in adolescents. After missing the entire first semester, Judy transferred to New York University in the spring. She enjoyed life in Greenwich Village with its art galleries and cafes. While on Christmas vacation her sophomore year, Judy met John Blume, a 25-year-old lawyer. A year later, they decided to get married.

According to Jewish custom, a wedding is never canceled due to a death in the family. So, when Judy's father suffered a heart attack before her wedding in the summer of 1959, he whispered to Judy, "This is the wrong time," just before he died. Judy was devastated.

A year later when she graduated from the School of Education at NYU, Judy was pregnant with her first child. Her daughter Randy was born in 1961 and a son, Larry, two years later. At age 25, Judy had everything she had thought she ever wanted: a successful husband, two healthy children, and a nice house in the New Jersey suburbs.

Yet, there was an emptiness in Judy's life because she had no outlet for her creativity. As soon as both of her children were in nursery school, Judy began to seek out a career for herself in the arts.

At first, Judy tried song writing. She soon switched to making colorful felt banners for children's rooms, which she sold and enjoyed some success with until she became allergic to the glue she was using. Judy then began to write children's picture books, which she illustrated herself and submitted to publishers. When Judy received her first rejection slip, she hid in a closet to cry. Then she signed up for a writing class at NYU.

While attending this course, Judy published her first two short stories. Soon after, she published her first book, *The One in the Middle Is a Green Kangaroo* (1969), a book for young children.

Blume autographs one of her many books for an appreciative reader.

While still attending the NYU writing class, Judy began to write *Iggie's House,* a novel about a black family who move into an all-white neighborhood. Judy bravely submitted a draft of her novel to Bradbury Press when she read that this small publishing company was looking for realistic fiction for young people. To her surprise, Bradbury Press expressed interest in *Iggie's House*–if she was willing to revise it.

Judy worked on the rewrite of her manuscript for a month before resubmitting it to Bradbury Press. They decided to publish the book and told her how impressed they were with her willingness to work with them, to listen and revise in order to create a better book . "I wrote my first book from the outside," Judy explained later.

Are You There God? It's Me, Margaret was the first book Judy wrote from deep inside herself–where the best books come from. She began to write from her own experiences, telling exactly what it feels like to be a preteenager growing up with lots of questions and secrets and no one to talk to about them. This meant writing about sex and sexual development, religion and God, social and family relationships, but from a kid's point of view. This type of book had never been written before: a book intended for young people, about young people, and about what really concerns young people. It took Judy only six weeks to write the first draft of *Are You There God? It's Me, Margaret* because she remembered so clearly what it felt like to be in sixth grade. Judy says now, "In Margaret, I just let go and wrote what I wanted to write and told the truth about what I felt."

It worked. Book reviewers and critics had not liked *Iggie's House* when it was released in 1970, and even Judy knew it was just a beginner's attempt. But the critics had high praise for *Are You There God? It's Me, Margaret,* which was selected as one of the *New York Times* outstanding children's books of that same year.

However, some schools banned *Margaret* because of the subject matter: The protagonist is a 12-year-old girl, and the novel reads like a young girl's diary, full of discussion about budding breasts, menstrual periods, boys, parents, and God. Such "adult" subject matter had long been regarded as off-limits in books written for young people, even though young people must confront such issues every day in their personal lives. When Judy sent several copies of *Margaret* to her own children's school, the principal there refused to place them on the library shelf.

Kids read the book anyway. Many wrote letters to Judy. "You don't know me but you wrote this

Blume (right) puts her fame to work for causes she believes in, including women's issues and intellectual freedom.

book about me, and I am Margaret," one 12-year-old girl wrote to Judy.

Judy soon became a best-selling author. Her 22 books (to date) have sold more than 65 million copies worldwide, and have been translated into 20 languages. She has been awarded many honors, including Most Admired Author, the Parent's Choice Award, and the Civil Liberties Award for promoting freedom of speech.

Judy's ideas for her books, the characters and events, are often based on her own life and experiences. Following her first divorce in 1975 and her remarriage in 1976, Judy and her family moved to Los Alamos, New Mexico. But this marriage too was troubled, and three years later Judy found herself divorced again. She wrote about the difficulties of marriage in her first adult novel, *Wifey* (1978), and of single parenting and remarriage in two more adult novels, *Smart Women* (1984) and *Summer Sisters* (1998). Through the most difficult years, Judy recalls, "I think writing saved me."

For nearly two decades Judy has been happily married to George Cooper, a fellow writer who supports and understands her commitment to her work. And Judy has enjoyed her relationship with George's daughter, Amanda. All of these life changes have provided Judy with more experiences for use in her writing.

In 1996, the American Library Association presented Judy with their Margaret A. Edwards Award for lifetime achievement, young adult literature's highest honor. The association specifically cited her for her 1975 book, *Forever . . .*, Judy's most controversial publication. In writing about a high school girl who falls in love and enters into her first sexual relationship, Judy broke new ground in young adult literature. Although many libraries banned the book, millions of teenagers have read *Forever . . .* and appreciated its truth.

With the publication of her most recent book, *Summer Sisters*, Judy brings to the adult experience of an intense friendship between two women the same direct, accessible writing she has so frequently shown in her children's books.

TONI MORRISON

When Toni Morrison was born on February 18, 1931, her parents named her Chloe Anthony Wofford. The second-oldest child in what was eventually a family of four children, Chloe grew up in the steel-mill town of Lorain, Ohio, during America's Great Depression. Unemployment was extremely high, but Chloe's father, George Wofford, worked three jobs to provide for his family.

When Chloe was 13, she worked after school as a cleaning girl for a local white family in order to help out with the Wofford's expenses. Despite their poor and difficult lives, the Woffords worked hard to make sure their children knew that they were important as individuals.

Many of Chloe's relatives passed along to her their knowledge of African-American folklore and mythology, introducing her to the traditional beliefs in spirits, visions, and signs. Storytelling was an important part of her home life. Her parents regularly told ghost stories. "We were intimate with the supernatural," Morrison would later say. Chloe's grandmother recorded her dreams in a special book. "I grew

Toni Morrison acknowledges tributes to her at a 1994 gathering of artists and performers.

up in a house in which people talked about their dreams with the same authority that they talked about what 'really' happened," Morrison recalled as an adult. Her parents also sparked her imagination with troubling and inspirational tales of her ancestors' experiences as slaves in the Old South. Chloe's mother, Ramah, often sang the Southern songs she had learned as a girl in Mississippi.

The Woffords lived in an integrated neighborhood, and Chloe attended school with children from many different cultures. She has memories of vivid examples of racial discrimination from her childhood, including white boys who threw rocks and a public park that was regarded as off-limits for black people. Chloe's mother often sat in protest in the restricted area ("whites only") of the local theater. And Chloe's uncles regularly brought lawsuits against people who demonstrated business-related prejudice, such as refusing to serve food to black people.

Chloe also spent a lot of time buried in books, learning to read before she began the first grade and advancing to the classics of European literature by the time she was a teenager. She was especially partial to the great Russian novelists, Dostoevski and Tolstoy, as well as to the novels of British author Jane Austen. She was also a big fan of the American novelists Ernest Hemingway, William Faulkner, and Willa Cather.

After graduating from Lorain High School in 1949, Chloe was accepted at Howard University, a predominantly black school in Washington, D.C. She was the first female in her family to attend college. In order to help pay for the cost of her education, Ramah worked as a ladies' room attendant.

While at Howard, Chloe began to call herself "Toni" (from her middle name, Anthony) because the new people in her life seemed to have so much difficulty pronouncing "Chloe." She majored in English and became active in theater. As a member of the Howard University Players, Toni appeared in on-campus plays and traveled around the South giving performances to mostly black audiences.

When she graduated from Howard, Toni went on to Cornell University in Ithaca, New York, for a master of arts degree in English. She then taught English at Texas Southern University in Houston for a year and a half, returning to Howard University in 1957, this time as an English teacher.

While teaching at Howard, Toni met and married Harold Morrison, a young architect of Jamaican descent. The marriage was troubled, and Toni prefers not to discuss it publically, except to say the problems came from cultural differences.

It was during this difficult time in her life that Toni began to write stories: "It was as though I had nothing left but my imagination. I had no will, no judgment, no perspective, no power, no authority, no self–just . . . a trembling respect for words. I wrote like someone with a dirty habit. Secretly. Compulsively. Slyly."

Toni joined a writers' group that met once a month in Washington, D.C. Group members read and critiqued one another's work. She attended for the social life more than from any real desire to become a serious writer, enjoying the company of poets and writers who loved literature as much as she did. It was for the group that Toni wrote a story about a black girl who wished for blue eyes. The idea for the story came from a memorable conversation she had as a child with another girl, who said she did not believe in God because her two years of prayers for blue eyes had never been answered.

When Toni resigned from her position at Howard

in 1964, she was pregnant with her second child. She traveled to Europe that summer with Harold and their eldest boy, Harold Ford, whom they called Ford. After the trip, Harold returned to Jamaica and Toni went home to her family in Lorain, where her second son, Slade, was born. Later, the Morrisons were divorced.

Toni soon landed a job with a company in Syracuse, New York. She was hired as an associate editor for a textbook subsidiary of Random House, specifically to develop school texts that addressed the African-American experience, which had been largely ignored by historians, writers, and educators. While in Syracuse, Toni began to expand her story about the girl who wanted blue eyes into a novel. She recalled later, "I had two small children in a strange place and I was very lonely. Writing was something for me to do in the evenings, after the children were asleep."

By 1967, Toni was working as a senior editor at the New York City office of Random House, using her influence to help black writers get their work published. She also continued to develop her novel, *The Bluest Eye,* depicting what it was like to grow up black and female in America. "I was really writing a book I wanted to read . . . I hadn't seen a book in which black girls were center stage," Toni explained later. The theme of the book is black self-hatred in a society that values whiteness as the only acceptable form of beauty.

In creating *The Bluest Eye,* Toni was developing her special "signature" writing style: a mixture of fantasy and reality that draws on African-American myths and legends. By presenting elegantly the music of ordinary black talk through vivid narration and lively dialogue, Morrison uses language to express the black experience in all of its beauty and suffering.

The Bluest Eye gave voice to the ordinary American black girls who had stories to tell. Toni Morrison brought public attention to the lives of black women, the problems and burdens, joys and special relationships between them. The novel received much critical attention, and Toni was soon hard at work on her next novel. "*Sula* was created out of the feeling that the way black women related to one another was different from the way white women related." In 1975, *Sula* was nominated for an important literary award, the National Book Award, bringing Toni national recognition.

When Toni published her third novel, *Song of Solomon,* her life took a new turn: The book became a best-seller and sold more than three million copies. *Song of Solomon* also won the 1977 National Book Critics Circle Award, a high honor, and became the first novel by a black writer in almost 40 years to serve as a Book-of-the-Month Club selection.

Toni cut back on her duties at Random House after editing the acclaimed anthology, *The Black Book,* covering 300 years of African-American life. Her next novel, *Tar Baby,* was an immediate best-seller, and Toni appeared on the March 30, 1981, cover of *Newsweek* magazine, the first black woman in the publication's history to be so honored.

In 1983, Toni finally left her position at Random House to focus solely on her writing. Soon she was back in the academic world, first at the State University of New York in Albany, and later at Princeton University, where she accepted the celebrated Robert F. Goheen Chair, becoming the first African-American writer to hold a named chair at an Ivy League university.

By this time, her most acclaimed book had been published: *Beloved,* for which Morrison was award-

Morrison's 1987 novel Beloved *deals with the legacies of slavery for African-Americans.*

In accepting the 1993 Nobel Prize for Literature from the king of Sweden, Morrison became the first African-American to be so honored.

ed the esteemed Pulitzer Prize for fiction, depicts how blacks are haunted, physically and spiritually, by their legacy of slavery. A film version of the book, released in October 1998, starred Oprah Winfrey.

In 1992, Toni published *Jazz,* another critically acclaimed novel, as well as a book of literary criticism, *Playing in the Dark: Whiteness and the Literary Imagination,* based on a series of lectures she had given at Howard University. Both books made the *New York Times* best-seller list that spring. It is very rare for a single author to have two books in two different categories on the best-seller list at the same time.

In 1993, Toni Morrison became the first African-American to receive the Nobel Prize in the area of literature. In an interview, she described what it felt like to be so honored, explaining that she was most pleased that her success could inspire young black Americans.

Her seventh novel, *Paradise,* is the third in a series of books chronicling the African-American experience since the 1800s (following *Beloved* and *Jazz*).

A prominent and respected figure in the field of literature, Toni Morrison continues to write stories that "mean something," sharing with readers her lyrical perspective on "how and why we learn to live this life intensely and well."

ALICE WALKER

When Alice Walker was born, the midwife charged her family three dollars. The youngest of eight children, Alice was the first baby for whom her father paid cash—the other births were paid for with pigs.

It was February 9, 1944, and the Walkers lived in Eatonton, Georgia, where Willie Lee Walker, Alice's father, was a sharecropper. Surviving on less than $300 a year, the Walkers moved from landowner to landowner to work the fields, making their home in small shacks.

An unusually bright and outgoing child, Alice began the first grade at the age of four. When she was eight, one of her older brothers accidently shot her in the right eye with a BB gun. She lost sight in that eye, which became disfigured with scar tissue. Her natural self-confidence waned, and little Alice became shy and lonely. "I couldn't look at people directly because I thought I was ugly," she recalled as an adult.

However, her half-blindness and the accompanying shyness caused Alice to become acutely sensitive to her environment. She became a keen observer of people, carefully

With the courage to tackle controversial subjects, Alice Walker overcame poverty and disability to become a successful writer.

studying their interactions and relationships. Her shyness also served her well, as young Alice spent a great deal of time reading books. "Jane Eyre [of the British literature classic of the same name] was my friend for a long time," Alice recalls. "Books became my world because the world I was in was very hard."

As a child, Alice enjoyed listening to her parents' stories, which she copied into a notebook. She also began to write poems in her notebook: "They were horrible poems, but they were poems," she said later. Writing helped her to feel less alone, and Alice soon decided she would become a writer.

Alice spent the summer of her 14th year in Boston with her older brother Bill and his family. Bill arranged for her to undergo surgery to correct the scarring in her eye. Afterward, she felt confident again: "I was a changed person. I promptly went home, scooped up the best-looking guy, and by the time I graduated from high school, I was Valedictorian, voted 'Most Popular,' and crowned Queen!" By 1962, Alice had also become involved in the civil rights movement and was a vocal advocate of the message of brotherhood promoted by civil rights leader Dr. Martin Luther King Jr.

With a disability scholarship from the Georgia Department of Rehabilitation (because of the blindness in her eye) and an academic scholarship from Spelman College in Atlanta, Alice was able to go to college.

While in school at Spelman, an all-black college, Alice began to write poetry in earnest, publishing some poems in the campus magazine. She was very active in the politics of the time, often participating in peace demonstrations and civil rights marches. She marched through Washington, D.C., in August 1963 when Martin Luther King Jr. delivered his famous "I Have a Dream" speech, in which he encouraged all African-Americans to work for change.

After two years, Alice transferred to Sarah Lawrence College in New York where, for the first time, she lived in "an almost totally white society." She continued to write poetry and began to explore fiction in the form of short stories.

In East Africa, where she had traveled on a fellowship, Alice dove into her senior year in college. Alice wrote poetry night and day. She wrote poems about the rich colors of Africa, poems on love and suicide, poems describing the marches of the civil rights movement. She shared these poems with her teacher, Muriel Rukeyser, who was an accomplished poet. Recognizing at once the beauty and genius in Alice's work, Rukeyser sent the poems on to New York, and eventually to an editor at what would become Alice's publisher. Three years later, Alice Walker's first poetry collection, *Once*, was published by Harcourt Brace Jovanovich. The book sold quickly, proving to be an immediate success.

In the meantime, Rukeyser sent Alice's short story "To Hell with Dying" to the well-known African-American writer Langston Hughes, who published it in his anthology, *Best Short Stories by Negro Writers.* Many years later, the story was republished as an illustrated children's book.

Upon graduating from Sarah Lawrence, Alice invested herself full-time in social justice work. She registered black voters in Georgia, then worked for the New York City Welfare Department. In 1966, with her first writing grant (provided by foundations to writers who show unusual talent), Alice was able to stop working and spend all of her time writing.

For inspiration, Alice chose to move to Mississippi, the focal point for some of the worst racial violence that had come to define the civil rights movement in the South during the '60s. She fell in love with a white law student working for the movement, and returned to New York with him for his last year of law school. Mel Leventhal was supportive of Alice's writing, and the two were married on March 17, 1967.

When Mel graduated from law school, they returned to Mississippi. Mel found work as a civil rights lawyer, while Alice instructed teachers on presenting African-American history to their classes. A state law at the time mandated that interracial couples could not live under one roof, and violent acts of racial discrimination were frequent. The couple bought a large dog and leaned a rifle by the front door.

Inspired by the stories of the Southern black women she was teaching, Alice wrote more poems and short stories. She also wrote essays and continued to work on a novel she had started back in New York. Writing helped her to deal with feelings of depression following the assassination of Dr. King in 1968, and the miscarriage she suffered only a week after she and Mel attended King's massive public funeral in Atlanta.

In 1969, Alice finished her first novel, *The Third Life of Grange Copeland,* and gave birth to her daughter Rebecca three days later. Walker's first book of fiction–like the novels that followed–is mainly concerned with what she regards as "exploring the oppressions, the insanities, the loyalties and the triumph of black women." According to Walker, "The black woman is one of America's greatest heroes. . . . Not enough credit has been given to the black woman who has been oppressed beyond recognition." She uses her writing to illustrate "the spirit that we see in black women."

With the publication of *Grange Copeland,* Alice Walker began to receive both the widespread public acclaim and the sometimes scathing criticism which continues to this day. Universally praised for their beautiful prose and memorable characters, Walker's books are highly controversial because of her portrayal of black men as violent and mostly unsympathetic oppressors of black women.

In doing some research for a short story she was writing, Alice discovered the work of the then obscure African-American writer Zora Neale Hurston. A collector of black folklore during the 1920s and '30s, Hurston had written two books on the topic, as well as four novels and an autobiography. So when Alice accepted a teaching position at Wellesley College in Wellesley, Massachusetts, she had the students in her course on African-American women writers read her favorite Hurston novel, *Their Eyes Were Watching God.* (This was the first time anyone had ever taught such a course. Walker taught it at the University of Massachusetts in Boston as well.)

In 1973, Alice tracked down Zora Neale Hurston's unmarked grave in Fort Pierce, Florida. Critically attacked during the 1940s and '50s, Hurston's work was shunned, and the author died in poverty in 1960. Alice bought a headstone, which she had engraved with the following words: "Zora Neale Hurston: 'A Genius of the South.'" After putting the marker on Hurston's grave, Alice published an essay in *Ms* magazine about the experience. Along with her classes and a collection of Hurston's work that she edited, Walker's article sparked public and academic interest in the neglected black author. Today, Zora Neale Hurston is widely read, her books commonly included in anthologies and in literature coursework.

Alice credits her research on Hurston for providing the courage she herself needed to continue

Walker shares a funny moment with her daughter Rebecca, to whom she dedicated her 1984 book In Search of Our Mothers' Gardens.

writing what she believed in, despite the harshness of her critics. Disparaged for being outspoken at a time when neither blacks nor women were supposed to speak their minds, Hurston refused to be silenced.

By 1976, Mel and Alice were divorced. Alice has not discussed the split publically. That same year, Walker's second novel was published. *Meridian* is often cited as the best novel written about the civil rights movement. The book is included in some American history courses, as well as being taught in literature classes. Since the life of the protagonist resembles Walker's own life in certain respects, she has been asked if the book is autobiographical. Walker explains that there is a part of herself in each of the characters she creates: "I'm everywhere and I'm everybody. That's true in all my books."

Walker talks with Robert Allen before a screening of the film version of The Color Purple *in Georgia in early 1986.*

Two more collections of Alice Walker's poetry were published before she began to work on a new novel, the book that would make her famous.

Although her work is regularly criticized for presenting an overly negative view of black men, Alice Walker often creates male characters who do eventually reform their violent, sexist ways. In *The Color Purple,* her third novel, the theme once again is the black woman's struggle for independence in the face of black male oppression. But the book is also full of humor and hope.

Told in a series of letters from and to the protagonist, Celie, *The Color Purple* is the story of one African-American woman's survival of sexual abuse and other acts of cruelty while growing up in the South from the 1920s to the 1940s. The character Celie is actually based on Alice's great-great-grandmother, a slave who was raped by her owner and had his child when she was only 11 years old. The character Shug is partly based on the personality of

Walker at work in 1984.

Zora Neale Hurston. All of the characters speak in what Walker refers to as "black folk English."

The Color Purple was a huge success, on the *New York Times* bestseller list for more than 25 weeks. The novel was nominated for the National Book Critics Circle Award in 1982 and won the American Book Award, a very prestigious literary prize, in 1983. When *The Color Purple* received a Pulitzer Prize that same year, Alice Walker became the first African-American woman to win the coveted prize in the area of fiction.

In 1985, Hollywood director Steven Spielberg's feature film version of *The Color Purple* opened to much fanfare and controversy. Picketers haunted the Los Angeles opening of the movie, and critics blasted it for the negative portrayal of black men. Walker, however, was pleased that the film brought public attention to issues of domestic violence.

From her home in Northern California, Alice Walker continues to publish inspirational works of poetry, fiction, and nonfiction. Her 1993 book, *Warrior Marks: Female Genital Mutilation and the Sexual Blinding of Women,* followed her highly praised novel on the same taboo subject, *Possessing the Secret of Joy.* Both books focus on circumcision of young girls to painfully protect their virginity and ensure their value in the marriage trade, a custom that is still widespread in the Middle East, Southeast Asia, and Africa. Walker and others brought widespread attention to a practice they see as torture.

Alice Walker stimulates the minds and hearts of

her readers with her unique blend of political activism and the art of storytelling. Her books have sold nearly 10 million copies and have been translated into more than two dozen languages. Like Zora Neale Hurston, the writer who inspired her, Alice Walker maintains her courage in the face of controversy and criticism. "I do understand that my worldview is different from that of most of the critics," she says. "I can only persist in being myself."

CHRONOLOGY

1650 Anne Bradstreet publishes *The Tenth Muse,* the first poetry collection published in the New World

1773 Phillis Wheatley's *Poems on Various Subjects* published in England

1852 Harriet Beecher Stowe publishes antislavery novel *Uncle Tom's Cabin*

1869 Louisa May Alcott's *Little Women* published

1890 First volume of Emily Dickinson's poetry published posthumously

1899 After controversial novel on women's sexual and emotional independence *The Awakening* published, author Kate Chopin's career ends

1905 Edith Wharton publishes first masterpiece, *The House of Mirth*

1918 First Pulitzer Prize for poetry awarded to Sara Teasdale

1921 Edith Wharton becomes first female to win Pulitzer Prize for fiction

1922 Willa Cather's novel *One of Ours* wins Pulitzer Prize

1931 Pearl S. Buck publishes *The Good Earth*

1933 Gertrude Stein publishes experimental work *The Autobiography of Alice B. Toklas*

1937 Zora Neal Hurston publishes *Their Eyes Were Watching God* during the Harlem Renaissance

1938 Pearl S. Buck becomes first American female to win Nobel Prize in literature

1966 Anne Sexton's *Live or Die,* poetry about her mental illness, published

1970 Judy Blume publishes her first popular young adult novel, *Are You There God? It's Me, Margaret*

1983 Alice Walker becomes first African-American female to receive Pulitzer Prize for fiction

1993 Toni Morrison becomes first African-American to win Nobel Prize in literature

FURTHER READING

Blume, Judy. *Letters to Judy: What Your Kids Wish They Could Tell You.* New York: Putnam, 1986.

Conn, Peter. *Pearl S. Buck: A Cultural Biography.* New York: Cambridge University Press, 1996.

Gilbert, Sandra M., and Susan Gubar. *The Norton Anthology of Literature by Women: The Tradition in English.* New York: Norton, 1985.

Kramer, Barbara. *Alice Walker: Author of "The Color Purple."* Springfield, N.J.: Enslow, 1995.

——. *Toni Morrison: Nobel Prize-Winning Author.* Springfield, N.J.: Enslow, 1996.

Leach, William. *Edith Wharton.* Philadelphia: Chelsea House, 1987.

Lee, Betsy. *Judy Blume's Story.* Minneapolis, Minn.: Dillon, 1981.

Lewis, R.W.B. *Edith Wharton: A Biography.* New York: Fromm International, 1985.

Patrick-Wexler, Diane. *Toni Morrison.* Austin, Tex.: Raintree Steck-Vaughn, 1997.

Sherrow, Victoria. *Phillis Wheatley: Poet.* Philadelphia: Chelsea House, 1992.

Walker, Alice. *In Search of Our Mothers' Gardens.* New York: Harcourt Brace Jovanovich, 1983.

——. *The Same River Twice: Honoring the Difficult.* New York: Scribner, 1996.

Weidt, Maryann N. *Revolutionary Poet: A Story About Phillis Wheatley.* Minneapolis, Minn.: Carolrhoda, 1997.

PHOTO CREDITS

AP/Wide World Photos: pp. 2, 23, 30; Library of Congress: pp. 10, 24; Corbis-Bettmann: p. 12; Schomburg Center for Research in Black Culture, Division of Photography and Prints/New York Public Library: p. 15; Archive Photos: p. 18; The Pearl S. Buck Foundation, by permission: pp. 26, 28; UPI/Corbis-Bettmann: p. 33; AP/Wide World Photos/Russell Landstrom: p. 34; Courtesy of Judy Blume: pp. 36, 38, 40; AP/Wide World Photos/Joseane Daher: p. 42; AP/Wide World Photos/Kathy Willens: p. 44; AP/Wide World Photos/David Bookstager: p. 49; Reuters/Archive Photos/Pressen Bild: p. 50; Corbis-Bettmann/Simon: p. 52; New York Times Co./Archive Photos/Sara Krulwich: pp. 58, 60; AP/Wide World Photos/Laura Sikes: p. 59.

INDEX

Age of Innocence, The (Wharton), 19, 23, 25
All Men Are Brothers (Buck, tr.), 35
Are You There, God? It's Me, Margaret (Blume), 41

Beloved (Morrison), 49–50, 51
Best Stories by Negro Writers (Hughes, ed.), 55
Black Book, The (Morrison, ed.), 49
Bluest Eye, The (Morrison), 48–49
Blume, John, 39, 42
Blume, Judy, 37–43
Buck, Carol, 31–32, 35
Buck, John Lossing, 30, 33
Buck, Pearl S., 27–35

Child Who Never Grew, The (Buck), 35
"Chinese Student Mind, The" (Buck), 31
"Chinese Woman Speaks, A" (Buck), 31–32
Codman, Jr., Ogden, 21
Color Purple, The (Walker), 59–60
Cooper, George, 42
Countess of Huntingdon, 13–14
Custom of the Country, The (Wharton), 22

Decoration of Houses, The (Codman and Wharton), 21, 25

Ethan Frome (Wharton), 22

"Farewell to America" (Wheatley), 15
Forever . . . (Blume), 43
Franklin, Benjamin, 15, 17
Fullerton, Morton, 22

Good Earth, The (Buck), 32
Greater Inclination, The (Wharton), 21

Hancock, John, 14
House of Mirth, The (Wharton), 22
Howard University, 47
Hughes, Langston, 55
Hurston, Zora Neale, 57, 60

Iggie's House (Blume), 40–41
In Search of Our Mothers' Gardens (Walker), 58
It's Not the End of the World (Blume), 42

James, Henry, 22
Jazz (Morrison), 50, 51

King Jr., Dr. Martin Luther, 54, 56

Leventhal, Mel, 56, 58

Margaret A. Edwards Award, 42
Meridian (Walker), 58
Morrison, Harold, 47
Morrison, Toni, 45–51

National Book Award, 49
National Book Critics Circle Award, 49, 60
Nobel Prize for literature, 33, 35, 50

Once (Walker), 55
One in the Middle Is a Green Kangaroo, The (Blume), 39
"On the Death of Rev. Dr. Sewell" (Wheatley), 13
Otherwise Known as Sheila the Great (Blume), 38

Paradise (Morrison), 51
Peters, John, 16–17
Playing in the Dark: Whiteness and the Literary Imagination (Morrison), 50
Poems on Various Subjects, Religious and Moral (Wheatley), 15–17
Possessing the Secret of Joy (Walker), 60
Pulitzer Prize for fiction, 23, 60

"Reply" (Wheatley), 17
Rhinelander, William, 19
Ruckeyser, Muriel, 55

Smart Women (Blume), 42
Song of Solomon (Morrison), 49
Starring Sally J. Freedman as Herself (Blume), 38
Sula (Morrison), 49
Summer Sisters (Blume), 42, 43

Tar Baby (Morrison), 49
Their Eyes Were Watching God (Hurston), 57
Third Life of Grange Copeland, The (Walker), 56
"To Hell with Dying" (Walker), 55
"To the University of Cambridge" (Wheatley), 13

Walker, Alice, 53–61
Walsh, Richard, 32–33, 35
Warrior Marks: Female Genital Mutilation and the Sexual Blinding of Women (Walker), 60
Washington, George, 16
Wharton, Edith, 19–25
Wharton, Edward, 21
Wheatley, Phillis, 11–17
Wifey (Blume), 42
Winfrey, Oprah, 50

ABOUT THE AUTHOR

Virginia Aronson is the author of more than a dozen books, including *The White House Family Cookbook,* coauthored with the former White House chef, and *Different Minds, Different Voices,* a collection of artwork by individuals with psychological disorders. She also writes books for young people, poetry, and plays.